Bon Jovi
Trivia Quiz Book

Copyright 2013,
All rights reserved.

Published by Mega Media Depot
P.O. Box 945
Prospect Heights, Il 60070

Manufactured in the United States of America

Some of the images in this book are used under the terms of agreement and paid subscription plans with Clipart.com and Fotolia.com.

Disclaimer

IMPORTANT: All information in this book is for news matter and entertainment purposes only and is not intended to be used in any direct or indirect violation of local, state, federal or international law(s). Any use of information and recommendations provided by this book is to be used at a visitor's sole discretion. The author, owner and publisher are not liable for any losses or damages incurred directly or indirectly.

Bon Jovi

Did bon Jovi start playing a guitar and piano in the year 1975?

Bon Jovi

Yes when he was only 13 years old

Bon Jovi

Did Bon Jovi form a band with Bryan?

Bon Jovi

Yes when he was 16 years old a band by the name Atlantic Expressway

Did Bon Jovi quit from playing in the band because he was still a teenager?

No he continued playing even in the local clubs

Did Bon Jovi form a band in the year 1980?

Bon Jovi

Yes he formed a band by the name the Rest which did open up for the acts in New Jersey

Did Bon Jovi take a job at the Power station studio?

Bon Jovi

Yes in the year 1982 when ha had finished school

Bon Jovi

Did Bon Jovi take any part time work when he finished his school?

Bon Jovi

Yes he was working at the women's shoe store

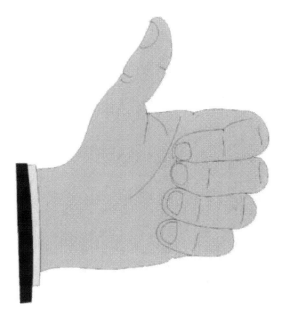

Bon Jovi

Did Bon Jovi write a song called jingles and also did sing it?

Bon Jovi

Yes in the year 1983 when he did visit a local radio station

Bon Jovi

Did the idea of having the bon Jovi's band in the year 1984 as Johnny electric succeed?

Bon Jovi

No since the group suggested the album to be called Bon Jovi

Bon Jovi

Was this album by Bon Jovi their success to record it?

No but it was McGhee who was the new manager who helped them

Was Bon Jovi's second album Fahrenheit?

Bon Jovi

Yes and it was released in the year 1985

Bon Jovi

Did Bon Jovi release any album in the year 1986?

Bon Jovi

Yes, on 16th august the album slippery when wet was on air

Bon Jovi

Did Bon Jovi release any album in the year 1988?

Bon Jovi

Yes in September the year 1988 he released the
New Jersey which did peak in the UK and the US

Bon Jovi

Did Bon Jovi record a solo album?

Bon Jovi

Yes between the year 1990 and 1991

Bon Jovi

Did any of Bon Jovi track win an award?

Bon Jovi

Yes in the year 1991 the track blaze of glory was awarded as the favorite pop single

Bon Jovi

Was the track blaze of glory by Bon Jovi awarded a golden globe?

Bon Jovi

Yes it was awarded during the music awards in America

Bon Jovi

Did Bon Jovi write and record any songs in the year 2012?

Bon Jovi

Yes where he did write and record the songs for a film by the name stand up guys

Bon Jovi

Did bon Jovi reunite in the year 1999?

Bon Jovi

Yes he did reunite to record a track called the real life

Bon Jovi

Was Bon Jovi awarded in the year 2004?

Bon Jovi

Yes, in November the year 2004 he was awarded an award for merit at the music awards in America

Bon Jovi

Was Bon Jovi working on anything in the year 2012?

Bon Jovi

Yes in January 2012 he was working on the 12th album.

Bon Jovi

Did Bon Jovi release a live video in 2012?

Bon Jovi

Yes on 27th November he did release a video album known as inside out

Made in the USA
Middletown, DE
28 December 2016